HOW TO INVEST FOR TEENAGERS

From Level 13 to Level 18 – Succeeding Life's Game with Expert Tips on Money, Habits, and Future Wealth

Jerry R. Schaefer

i

OTHER BOOKS BY SAME AUTHOR

1. HOW TO INVEST $10,000 INTO FINANCIAL FREEDOM
2. HOW TO BUDGET AND SAVE MONEY FOR BEGINNERS
3. THE PATH TO LONG-TERM INVESTMENT
4. FINANCIAL INDEPENDENCE WITH 70% SAVING
5. ONE YEAR TO FINANCIAL FREEDOM
6. INVESTING STRATEGIES FOR ANY BUDGET
7. FROM YOUR FIRST $100K
8. HOW TO INVEST FOR BEGINNERS

TABLE OF CONTENTS

INTRODUCTION

Welcome to the ultimate guide on teen investment—a journey designed to equip you with the knowledge and skills to level up your financial game from the age of 13 to 18. In the vast landscape of personal finance, this book serves as your trusted walkthrough, providing straightforward advice tailored to the unique challenges and opportunities that teenagers face.

1.1 Understanding the Teen Investment Journey

Embarking on the teen investment journey is like navigating through a video game of life. Just as in a game, you don't choose your character or starting stats—they're assigned to you randomly. However, you have control over your character's actions and decisions, much like how you control your life.

This book recognizes that if you've clicked on it, you're likely a Gen Z individual, a parent seeking advice for your kids, or perhaps someone who stumbled upon it during the late-night internet exploration. Regardless of the reason, you're in the right place.

Before diving into the intricacies of financial wisdom, let's address a common dilemma—millennials versus zoomers. There's banter about zoomers outshining millennials on TikTok, and it seems unfair. Millennials inherited a challenging economy, facing low job prospects and meager incomes. Boomers labeled them as entitled, and now, zoomers are seemingly piling on. It's essential to acknowledge these generational dynamics but also to approach the topic with a hint of humor.

Now, let's set aside the jokes and delve into the heart of this guide—investment advice tailored for teenagers. Whether you have $100 or $1,000 to invest, the key is to seek the highest returns possible. A crucial point emphasized here is the risk associated with the stock market. While potential gains exist, there's an equal chance of losing your initial investment. Instead, the book encourages investing in personal development during these early stages of life.

The book introduces the concept of life's currency—time. You can invest either money or time. In this early teen level, watching tutorials and learning from those who have navigated life's challenges, including teachers and experienced family members, becomes a valuable strategy.

1.2 The Importance of Starting Early

In the exhilarating realm of teen investing, where every decision shapes the trajectory of future wealth, a pivotal concept takes center stage: the unparalleled importance of starting early. This section delves into the profound impact that initiating the investment journey during the teen years can have on long-term financial success.

The Time Advantage

Time, often underestimated, emerges as the ultimate ally in the quest for financial prosperity. Starting the investment journey in the teen years provides a distinctive advantage — the luxury of time. As characters embark on their teen investment adventure, they step onto a path where every dollar invested holds the potential to multiply exponentially over the years.

The concept is rooted in the magical realm of compound interest. By planting the seeds of investment early, characters allow their money to grow not just on the initial principal but also on the accumulated interest from previous periods. This compounding effect is akin to a snowball rolling downhill, gaining size and momentum with every revolution. Starting early magnifies the impact of compounding, transforming modest investments into substantial wealth over time.

Building a Fortress of Financial Resilience

The teen years are a unique window of opportunity to fortify one's financial future. Early investors are afforded the luxury of weathering market fluctuations, economic cycles, and unforeseen challenges with resilience. This financial fortress, constructed through consistent and strategic investment practices, acts as a safeguard against the uncertainties that may arise in adulthood.

Moreover, the ability to absorb lessons from both successes and setbacks becomes a valuable asset. Starting early not only allows characters to accumulate wealth but also cultivates a robust financial mindset, honed through real-world experiences. This resilience, forged in the crucible of early investments, becomes an enduring companion as characters progress through different stages of life.

Seizing the Power of Long-Term Goals

The importance of starting early extends beyond the quantitative realm. It empowers characters to envision and pursue ambitious long-term goals. Whether aiming for homeownership, entrepreneurship, or a comfortable retirement, early investors have the advantage of aligning their financial strategies with expansive, visionary objectives.

By setting the wheels of wealth in motion during the teen years, characters can confidently navigate the complexities of adulthood, equipped with a financial foundation built on foresight and strategic planning. The journey becomes not just a pursuit of monetary gain but a deliberate and purposeful march toward a future imbued with financial security and freedom.

In conclusion, "The Importance of Starting Early" emerges as a guiding principle in the teen investment narrative. It unlocks the gates to a world where time becomes a powerful ally, compounding the fruits of early investments. The advantages extend beyond monetary gains, fostering resilience, and nurturing a mindset attuned to long-term goals. As characters embrace the wisdom of starting early, they embark on a journey that transcends immediate gains, laying the groundwork for a future where financial abundance and security abound.

Level 13: Getting Started

As you enter Level 13 on your teen investment journey, the initial challenge lies in deciding where to allocate your precious resources—your coins of time and energy. This level is a crucial juncture, emphasizing the foundational principle that investing in personal development is the key to unlocking long-term success in the complex game of life.

2.1 Investing in Personal Development

Consider personal development as the skill tree that shapes your character throughout the game. Just like in a video game, where leveling up certain attributes enhances your overall abilities, investing in personal development involves intentional actions aimed at boosting your skills, knowledge, and mindset.

At this stage, the concept of investing might evoke thoughts of financial ventures, but the focus here is on investing in yourself. It's about recognizing that your greatest asset is not the number of coins in your pocket but the skills and abilities you cultivate within. The returns on personal development are immeasurable, contributing to both your character's strength and resilience.

Start by exploring the vast landscape of knowledge available to you. Take advantage of the tutorials offered by the seasoned players in the game—the teachers, parents, and mentors who have accumulated valuable experience points. Devote time to understanding their strategies and learning from their successes and setbacks.

In this level, acquiring knowledge becomes your primary quest. Expand your horizons by reading books, exploring various subjects, and embracing a curious mindset. The value of a well-rounded education extends beyond the classroom, encompassing a continuous pursuit of wisdom in the ever-evolving game of life.

Beyond knowledge acquisition, hone your soft skills. Communication, critical thinking, and adaptability are like special abilities that can significantly enhance your gameplay. Engage in activities that challenge you to think creatively, solve problems, and communicate effectively. These skills are the tools that will serve you well in the diverse challenges that lie ahead.

Consider this level as the foundational stage for character building. It's about discovering your strengths and weaknesses, understanding your character's unique attributes, and strategically investing in skill points that align with your aspirations. Just as a well-equipped character navigates challenges more efficiently in a game, a well-rounded individual equipped with a diverse skill set can navigate the complexities of life more effectively.

While financial investments may come later in the game, investing in personal development is an ongoing quest that pays dividends throughout your entire journey. It sets the stage for future levels, creating a resilient character capable of adapting to the twists and turns that the game of life presents.

In conclusion, Level 13 introduces you to the fundamental concept that the most significant investment you can make is in yourself. As you navigate this level, embrace the opportunity to explore the skill tree of personal development, acquiring the knowledge and skills that will serve as the cornerstone for your success in the levels to come. Remember, in the game of life, a well-developed character is the ultimate asset.

2.2 Choosing the Right Investment for Teens

As you progress through Level 13 on your teen investment journey, the next pivotal decision revolves around choosing the right investment strategy. While the allure of the stock market may be tempting, this stage emphasizes the importance of understanding the options available and tailoring your investment choices to align with your unique goals, risk tolerance, and the evolving landscape of the game.

Investing at a young age is akin to selecting the right weapon or tool for your character in a video game. Each investment option carries its own set of attributes, risks, and potential rewards. It's not about choosing the most complex or trendy investment; rather, it's about selecting the one that aligns with your current resources and future aspirations.

One essential aspect to grasp at this level is the distinction between active and passive investing. Active investing involves hands-on management of your investments, often with a goal of outperforming the market. On the other hand, passive investing entails a more hands-off approach, typically through index funds or Exchange-Traded Funds (ETFs) that mirror the performance of a specific market index.

For beginners entering the investment realm, the book advises leaning towards passive investing. It's like opting for a versatile, reliable weapon in a game that ensures a steady and consistent performance. Passive investments, such as index funds, provide diversification, reducing the risk associated with putting all your coins into a single stock.

Diversification, much like having an array of skills in your character's arsenal, spreads the risk across different sectors and industries. It shields you from the impact of a poor-performing investment dragging down your overall progress. It's a strategy that aligns with the age-old adage of not putting all your eggs in one basket—a principle that remains relevant in the dynamic landscape of financial markets.

Moreover, the book introduces the concept of risk tolerance—a crucial factor in selecting the right investment. Understanding your risk tolerance is like determining your character's threshold for challenges in a game. If you're a risk-averse player, you might opt for more conservative investments that provide steady but moderate returns. Conversely, if you thrive on challenges and can weather market volatility, you might be inclined towards more aggressive investments with higher potential returns.

The goal at this level is not to accumulate wealth rapidly but to lay a solid foundation for future growth. Choosing the right investment strategy involves considering your investment horizon—the time you plan to keep your coins invested before needing them. For teens, having a longer investment horizon means there's more time to recover from market fluctuations and benefit from the compounding effects of returns.

In conclusion, Level 13 encourages teens to approach investment decisions with a strategic mindset. Much like selecting the ideal tools for a character's journey in a game, choosing the right investment involves understanding your options, embracing diversification, and aligning your choices with your risk tolerance and time horizon. As you navigate this level, remember that the right investment strategy is not a one-size-fits-all approach but a tailored decision that sets the stage for a successful and sustainable financial journey.

2.3 Exploring the Currency of Time

Time, the universal constant that ticks away, is an invaluable currency that holds unparalleled significance, especially for teenagers venturing into the realm of investing. In the intricate game of life, understanding the unique properties of time is pivotal, akin to unlocking a secret skill that sets the stage for financial success.

At Level 13, teenagers stand at the crossroads of adolescence, armed with a modest sum of coins and a thirst for exploration. This stage marks the beginning of the journey into the fascinating world of investments. However, what often goes unnoticed is the incredible power embedded in the currency of time. Unlike money, which can be earned, spent, and lost, time is a resource that, once spent, cannot be regained.

The early teen years offer a crucial window for teens to harness the potential of time in shaping their financial future. It is during this period that the compound interest, a magical force in the investment world, works most effectively. By putting even a small amount of money into investments, teens can witness the remarkable growth that occurs over time, thanks to the compounding effect.

Imagine a scenario where a teenager invests a modest sum at Level 13, and over the course of several years, that investment grows exponentially, outpacing what might be achieved by starting later in life. This is the power of allowing investments to marinate in the market, accumulating wealth over an extended period. The compounding effect transforms time into a strategic advantage, creating a financial snowball effect that gains momentum with each passing year.

The teen years are the prime time to leverage this advantage, as responsibilities and financial commitments are often minimal. While the allure of immediate gratification might tempt some to spend their coins on short-term pleasures, the wise investor recognizes the potential for long-term rewards by letting time work in their favor.

Furthermore, the lessons learned during these early stages extend beyond financial gains. Teens can use this time to invest in themselves, honing skills, acquiring knowledge, and developing a strong foundation for their future endeavors. Exploring different interests, engaging in educational pursuits, and building a diverse set of skills all contribute to the rich tapestry of personal development.

However, it's crucial to acknowledge that the currency of time is not infinite. The game of life comes with its own set of challenges and uncertainties, introducing an element of randomness (RNG) that cannot be controlled. Hence, the urgency to embark on this journey early, to capitalize on the favorable odds when the time is ripe.

In conclusion, exploring the currency of time is not just about making wise financial investments; it's about embracing the opportunities for growth and development that time presents. Teenagers, armed with the knowledge that time is on their side, can strategically navigate the intricate levels of life, making informed decisions that pave the way for a prosperous future. As they unlock the potential of time, they not only accumulate wealth but also shape a narrative that transcends the boundaries of financial success, encompassing a life well-lived and lessons well-learned.

Level 14: The Reading Quest

Embarking on Level 14 of your teen investment journey leads you to a pivotal stage—the Reading Quest. At this level, the importance of acquiring knowledge takes center stage, and the book "The Simple Path to Wealth" by J.L. Collins becomes your trusty guide, illuminating the path to financial wisdom in a language tailored for the budding adventurer.

3.1 The Simple Path to Wealth by J.L. Collins

The book serves as a treasure map, guiding you through the labyrinth of financial concepts with clarity and simplicity. Collins, a seasoned player in the game of wealth-building, imparts valuable insights that demystify the complexities of investing. Much like a seasoned mentor sharing wisdom with a novice, the author's approach is not laden with jargon but resonates with straightforward advice that resonates with readers of all levels.

The central tenet of "The Simple Path to Wealth" is the philosophy of simplicity and long-term thinking. Collins advocates for a straightforward approach to investing, emphasizing low-cost index funds as the primary tool in your financial arsenal. This concept is akin to selecting a reliable, versatile weapon in a game—something you can depend on in various scenarios without unnecessary complications.

The book introduces the concept of Financial Independence Retire Early (FIRE), which becomes a beacon on your quest. FIRE is not just about accumulating wealth but about gaining the freedom to shape your destiny, much like unlocking a special ability in a game that opens new realms of possibilities.

Collins shares his own experiences, weaving personal anecdotes into the narrative. This storytelling aspect adds a relatable dimension to the book, making it more than just a set of instructions. It becomes a companion on your journey, offering guidance through the author's own trials and triumphs.

As you delve into the pages of "The Simple Path to Wealth," you encounter the notion of embracing market volatility rather than fearing it. This is a strategic move in the game of investing—seeing market fluctuations not as obstacles but as opportunities to acquire assets at discounted prices. Collins encourages readers to adopt a resilient mindset, aligning with the understanding that the market's unpredictability is a natural element of the game.

Furthermore, the book provides valuable insights into the psychology of investing. Understanding the emotional aspects of financial decisions is akin to acquiring a skill that enhances your gameplay. Collins emphasizes the importance of staying the course during market downturns, a principle that echoes the resilience needed to navigate challenges in any quest.

In conclusion, Level 14's Reading Quest is a transformative stage in your teen investment journey. "The Simple Path to Wealth" serves as your beacon, guiding you through the intricacies of investing with a focus on simplicity and long-term thinking. Collins' narrative style transforms financial concepts into relatable lessons, making this book not just a guide but a companion on your quest for financial wisdom. As you absorb the wisdom within its pages, you equip yourself with the knowledge needed to navigate the evolving landscapes of the game of wealth-building.

3.2 I Will Teach You to Be Rich by Ramit Sethi

Ramit Sethi's book is a treasure trove of actionable advice, tailored to resonate with individuals navigating the complexities of personal finance. The title itself is a bold promise, setting the tone for a guide that aims not only to educate but to transform its readers into masters of their financial destinies.

Sethi's approach is characterized by a blend of practicality and humor, making the journey through financial concepts feel more like an engaging conversation than a lecture. He recognizes the diverse player base in the game of wealth-building and tailors his advice to suit various playstyles and preferences.

At the heart of "I Will Teach You to Be Rich" lies the concept of automating financial decisions—an ingenious strategy that aligns with the efficiency of optimizing character actions in a game. Sethi encourages readers to set up automated systems for saving, investing, and bill payments. This approach ensures that financial progress occurs seamlessly, much like background processes running in a game that enhance your character's capabilities.

The book addresses the importance of conscious spending, a concept analogous to strategic resource allocation in a game. Sethi advocates for focusing on expenditures that bring genuine joy and value, urging readers to cut back on mindless spending while splurging on experiences and items that contribute to a fulfilling life.

Sethi's emphasis on negotiating bills and optimizing credit card rewards is akin to uncovering hidden quests and secret passages in a game. It's about maximizing the utility of available resources, ensuring that every financial move contributes to your overall progress. The author provides practical scripts for negotiating, empowering readers to approach financial interactions with confidence.

Moreover, the book delves into the psychology of money, offering insights into the behavioral aspects of financial decision-making. Understanding the intricacies of one's relationship with money is akin to gaining insight into a character's motivations and preferences in a game. Sethi's exploration of these psychological nuances equips readers with the self-awareness needed to make sound financial choices.

"I Will Teach You to Be Rich" serves as more than just a manual—it's a dynamic playbook for achieving financial success. Sethi addresses the unique challenges faced by teens entering the financial arena, providing tailored advice that resonates with this specific player base. As you navigate this stage of the Reading Quest, Sethi's book becomes a mentor, offering guidance and strategies to level up your financial gameplay.

In conclusion, Level 14's Reading Quest reaches new heights with "I Will Teach You to Be Rich." Ramit Sethi's engaging approach and actionable advice transform financial concepts into tangible steps for teens entering the wealth-building game. As you absorb the wisdom within its pages, you not only gain financial knowledge but also acquire practical strategies to navigate the evolving landscapes of personal finance.

3.3 Advanced Reading: "The Intelligent Investor" by Benjamin Graham

Entering the world of Benjamin Graham is akin to stepping into a hallowed library of financial insights. Graham, often regarded as the father of value investing, imparts lessons that transcend the fleeting trends of the market, offering a strategic playbook for those seeking to master the complexities of the wealth-building game.

Graham introduces the concept of value investing— an advanced playstyle that involves identifying undervalued assets in the market. This approach is comparable to seeking legendary artifacts in a game—assets that possess intrinsic value overlooked by the majority of players. The book encourages a disciplined and patient approach to investing, urging readers to resist the allure of quick gains and focus on long-term stability.

One of the key tenets of "The Intelligent Investor" is the Margin of Safety—a powerful shield that protects your investments from the uncertainties of the market. Similar to gearing up with the best armor in a game, the Margin of Safety involves buying assets at a significant discount to their intrinsic value. This not only mitigates risks but also enhances the potential for substantial gains.

The book introduces the concept of Mr. Market—a whimsical character who personifies the market's erratic behavior. Graham's narrative skillfully likens the market to a capricious game companion, prone to emotional fluctuations. Understanding Mr. Market's nature is essential for any serious player, allowing you to navigate market volatility with a composed and strategic mindset.

Graham's emphasis on rationality and an analytical approach echoes the mindset required to solve intricate puzzles in a game. "The Intelligent

Investor" challenges readers to cultivate a mindset that transcends emotional reactions, fostering a disciplined approach to financial decision-making.

Moreover, the book explores the distinction between investing and speculation—a critical aspect often blurred in the fast-paced game of wealth-building. Graham's insights guide readers to differentiate between prudent, value-driven investing and speculative endeavors driven by market fads.

As you delve into the chapters of "The Intelligent Investor," you encounter the concept of the Defensive Investor and the Enterprising Investor—two archetypes that cater to different playstyles. Graham tailors his advice to suit the individual strengths and preferences of readers, recognizing that the wealth-building game accommodates various strategies.

In conclusion, "The Intelligent Investor" by Benjamin Graham is the advanced playbook in your Reading Quest, demanding a profound understanding of financial intricacies. As you navigate through the pages of this financial grimoire, you equip yourself with the tools and strategies needed to master the advanced levels of the wealth-building game. Graham's timeless wisdom becomes a guiding light, illuminating the path to financial mastery for those daring enough to undertake this ultimate challenge in the quest for wealth.

Levels 15-17: Evolving and Exploring Side Quests

As you ascend through Levels 15 to 17 in your teen investment journey, the game takes a transformative turn. This stage introduces opportunities for evolution and the exploration of side quests, unveiling crucial lessons and experiences that shape your character. One of the primary side quests that emerges during this phase is securing a job, offering insights into the value of money and initiating you into the real-world economy.

4.1 Getting a Job and Learning the Value of Money

Level 15 marks the initiation of a fundamental side quest—securing your first job. This experience is not just about earning in-game currency; it's a gateway to understanding the tangible value of money in the real world. Much like a character gaining experience points, every task and responsibility undertaken in your job contributes to your financial growth and understanding.

Acquiring a job at this level unveils a pivotal realization—the correlation between time, effort, and the money earned. It's a revelation that transcends the theoretical concepts encountered in earlier levels, providing a practical understanding of the economic forces at play. As you exchange your time and skills for a paycheck, you unlock a deeper appreciation for the value embedded in each dollar earned.

True to the essence of a side quest, this employment experience is not solely about accumulating wealth but also about grasping the concept of financial independence. It prompts you to contemplate personal goals and material aspirations, setting the stage for strategic planning in the wealth-building game.

A significant lesson gained from this side quest is the discernment of wants versus needs. Much like a character discerning essential items from mere trinkets in a game, the employment journey teaches you to allocate your earnings wisely. It reinforces the importance of mindful spending, encouraging you to prioritize necessities while recognizing the allure of discretionary expenses.

Between Levels 15 and 17, the narrative introduces the concept of side quests beyond the realm of traditional employment. These include diverse explorations—be it trying your hand at YouTube, TikTok, cooking, tennis, or even delving into the realms of magic cards, Photoshop, and photography. These side quests serve a dual purpose—they offer a glimpse into potential passion areas and act as avenues for discovering your master skill.

These endeavors, although seemingly unrelated to the primary quest of wealth-building, are akin to unlocking special abilities. They contribute to the overall character development, enhancing your skill set and opening doors to unforeseen opportunities. In the wealth-building game, finding your passion or mastering a valuable skill can be a game-changer, exponentially impacting your financial journey.

The side quests during Levels 15-17 are not only about accumulating in-game achievements but also about shaping your character's identity. Exploring diverse activities cultivates a broad skill tree, offering a strategic advantage in the long-term game of life. It's an invitation to discover your unique abilities and potentially unearth a cheat code that propels you ahead in the wealth-building quest.

In conclusion, Levels 15-17 unfold as a transformative phase, introducing the critical side quest of securing a job. This experience unveils the tangible value of money, providing practical insights into the dynamics of earning and spending. Moreover, the exploration of diverse side quests during this stage lays the foundation for character development, offering the potential to discover passion areas and master valuable skills. As you evolve through these levels, the wealth-building game expands its horizons, inviting you to navigate not only financial landscapes but also the intricate realms of personal growth and skill acquisition.

4.2 Exploring Passion Through Various Activities

In the vast landscape of the wealth-building game, engaging in various activities at this juncture serves as a compass, guiding you towards potential areas of passion and expertise. These side quests are akin to unlocking special abilities, each contributing to the expansion of your character's skill tree. The significance lies not just in the immediate rewards but in the long-term advantages these explorations can provide.

The narrative introduces YouTube and TikTok as platforms for self-expression and content creation. Venturing into these realms is comparable to embarking on a creative quest, where you learn to wield the tools of video production and storytelling. Much like mastering a new spell or combat technique in a game, these skills enhance your overall character proficiency.

Cooking, another avenue explored in this side quest, isn't merely about preparing meals; it's a journey into the alchemy of flavors and culinary arts. This exploration mirrors the strategic approach of gathering ingredients and following recipes, much like assembling resources and navigating challenges in a game.

Tennis, a physical pursuit in the repertoire of side quests, contributes to both your character's physical well-being and strategic agility. In the wealth-building game, physical health is an invaluable asset, impacting your overall performance and resilience against unexpected challenges.

Venturing into the realms of magic cards and Photoshop unveils the artistry within the game. These side quests are akin to acquiring proficiency in crafting or design, offering a creative outlet that can be monetized or leveraged in unexpected ways. Just as characters with diverse skills are sought after in a game, your unique talents become assets in the real-world economy.

Photography, a captivating side quest, teaches you to capture moments and tell stories through visuals. This skill is more than a hobby; it's a tool that enhances your communication abilities, much like leveling up a character's charisma in a game. In the wealth-building journey, effective communication is essential for networking, negotiation, and building fruitful connections.

Exploring these diverse activities isn't just about accumulating experiences; it's about uncovering your master skill or passion. The wealth-building game rewards those who can identify their unique strengths and apply them strategically. These side quests become a means of discovering your character's inherent abilities and aligning them with your overarching goals.

In conclusion, Levels 15-17 unfold as a phase of self-discovery through diverse activities. Exploring passions in YouTube, TikTok, cooking, tennis, magic cards, Photoshop, and photography enriches your character's skill set. Each side quest offers not only immediate rewards but also the potential to unveil your master skill. As you navigate these diverse pursuits, the wealth-building game transforms into a journey of personal growth, equipping you with a robust skill tree that enhances your overall capabilities in the evolving landscape of life.

4.3 The Importance of Discovering Your Master Skill

In the vast tapestry of the wealth-building game, discovering your master skill is akin to unearthing a hidden treasure—a unique ability or talent that, when honed, can catapult your character to unparalleled heights. This quest is not about conforming to predefined roles but about embarking on a journey of self-discovery, where each side quest and exploration serves as a piece of the puzzle in unraveling your inherent strengths.

The wealth-building game, much like a labyrinthine maze, presents myriad paths and choices. Without a compass or a guiding star, navigating this maze can be overwhelming. Discovering your master skill acts as that guiding star, providing clarity and purpose to your journey. It's the realization that you possess a unique attribute, a talent that, when cultivated, becomes a powerful tool in your arsenal.

Identifying your master skill involves introspection, experimentation, and a willingness to embrace the unknown. The side quests explored during Levels 15-17—YouTube, TikTok, cooking, tennis, magic cards, Photoshop, and photography—serve as potential avenues for uncovering this hidden treasure. Each activity offers a glimpse into your affinity, igniting the spark that could evolve into your master skill.

Consider the game of life as a grand tournament where individuals showcase their unique abilities. Your master skill becomes your signature move, the special ability that distinguishes you in the eyes of both allies and adversaries. It's not just a means to accumulate wealth; it's a strategic advantage that propels you forward in the competitive realms of the real-world economy.

The importance of discovering your master skill is magnified by its impact on your career trajectory. Aligning your profession with your inherent strengths isn't merely a strategy; it's a game-changing move. Just as a character excels when equipped with the right gear, your career gains momentum when fueled by your master skill.

Moreover, the quest for your master skill is intertwined with personal fulfillment and satisfaction. Much like completing a challenging quest in a game, uncovering your unique talent brings a sense of achievement and purpose. This intrinsic motivation becomes a driving force, influencing not only your career choices but also your overall well-being.

In conclusion, the importance of discovering your master skill transcends the confines of the wealth-building game. It's a quest that defines your character's identity and empowers you to navigate the maze of life with purpose and clarity. As you delve into the side quests during Levels 15-17, pay heed to the sparks of affinity and passion—they may lead you to the treasure trove of your master skill. Embrace the journey of self-discovery, for in your unique abilities lies the key to unlocking unparalleled success in the ever-evolving game of life.

Level 18: Essential Items for Success

As you ascend to Level 18 in the teen investment journey, the game introduces a pivotal stage marked by the acquisition of essential items crucial for long-term success. Among these indispensable assets, none stands more paramount than the initiation of a strategic move—opening a bank account with high-interest savings.

5.1 Opening a Bank Account with High-Interest Savings

Upon reaching Level 18, the game undergoes a significant shift, transitioning from the exploratory phases to a focused pursuit of foundational elements that will set the stage for the entirety of your play style. At the forefront of this strategic move is the imperative task of opening a bank account equipped with high-interest savings.

This quest is more than a routine financial transaction; it's a deliberate choice that aligns with the principles of compound interest—a powerful force within the wealth-building game. The selection of the right bank and savings account is akin to choosing your character's primary gear in preparation for a challenging quest.

Two prominent contenders in this realm are Ally Bank and CIT Bank, both renowned for offering high-interest rates on savings accounts. The decision between them involves assessing the fluctuating economic landscape, influenced by the final boss—the Federal Reserve. Understanding that these rates can vary is crucial, ensuring that the chosen bank remains aligned with your long-term wealth-building strategy.

The primary advantage of parking your money in a high-interest savings account lies in the concept of compound interest. It's not merely a storage space for your in-game currency; it's a mechanism that allows your money to grow passively over time. This growth compounds exponentially, creating a steady stream of income that augments your financial standing in the game.

While the immediate returns might seem modest, the true power of high-interest savings unfolds over the long term. It's a strategic move that capitalizes on the principle of time—the earlier you commence, the greater the impact. This aligns with the overarching theme of the wealth-building game, where time becomes a valuable currency, often more potent than the in-game currency itself.

Choosing to open a bank account with high-interest savings at Level 18 symbolizes a shift towards financial prudence and a keen understanding of the game's mechanics. It's a move that echoes the importance of utilizing every available resource for maximum advantage. Just as characters equip themselves with the best gear for upcoming challenges, you fortify your financial arsenal with a high-interest savings account.

This quest is not merely about accumulating wealth; it's a strategic maneuver that complements the overarching goal of securing financial stability and prosperity. The wealth-building game rewards foresight and wise decision-making, and opening a high-interest savings account aligns seamlessly with these principles.

In conclusion, Level 18 marks a pivotal stage in the teen investment journey, where the focus shifts from exploration to strategic acquisition. Opening a bank account with high-interest savings becomes a cornerstone move, aligning with the principles of compound interest and leveraging time as a valuable asset. This quest sets the stage for long-term success, embodying the essence of the wealth-building game—strategic decision-making, foresight, and the accumulation of resources for a prosperous future.

5.2 Building Credit with Responsible Credit Card Use

Entering the realm of Level 18 introduces a key aspect of the wealth-building game—the intricate mechanics of credit. Unlike a physical item or currency, credit is an intangible yet potent resource that can shape the trajectory of your financial journey. Building credit through responsible credit card use becomes a pivotal quest, with far-reaching implications for your character's economic prowess.

The first item on this quest list is obtaining a credit card, a powerful tool that, when wielded with care, can unlock a plethora of benefits. While the idea of credit cards might evoke cautionary tales, understanding their strategic use is akin to acquiring a legendary weapon in the game—one that, if handled wisely, can significantly enhance your character's capabilities.

A notable recommendation is the secured credit card, a prudent choice for those at Level 18 who are just stepping into the credit arena. The Discover it Secured card, for instance, serves as a reliable ally in this quest. It not only provides a gateway to credit but also offers cash back rewards—a dual benefit that aligns with the game's principle of maximizing returns on every move.

Building credit through responsible credit card use involves a strategic approach, emphasizing two primary principles: timely payments and prudent utilization. The credit game, much like the wealth-building game, rewards consistency and responsible decision-making. By ensuring that you pay your credit card bills on time, you not only avoid penalties but also showcase your character's reliability in handling financial responsibilities.

The second aspect, prudent utilization, involves maintaining a balance between credit usage and credit limit. Keeping your credit utilization rate low—ideally below 30%—demonstrates fiscal responsibility, a trait highly regarded in the game. This careful management of credit resources contributes to the gradual enhancement of your character's credit score.

Understanding the symbiotic relationship between credit cards and credit scores is paramount. A high credit score becomes a formidable asset, opening doors to favorable interest rates, premium financial opportunities, and increased trust from in-game financial institutions. It's a strategic move that positions your character as a reliable player in the economic landscape.

While the credit game may seem intricate, the rewards are substantial. A high credit score becomes a catalyst for future quests, such as acquiring loans for significant in-game assets like a house or car. It's an investment in your character's financial future, echoing the overarching theme of the wealth-building game—strategic decision-making for long-term prosperity.

In conclusion, Level 18 introduces the quest of building credit through responsible credit card use—a task often underestimated but crucial for long-term success. Choosing the right credit card, adhering to timely payments, and managing credit utilization strategically all contribute to the gradual enhancement of your character's credit score. This quest serves as a foundational move, positioning your character as a reliable and responsible player in the intricate game of credit and finance.

5.3 Starting a Retirement Account for Long-Term Wealth

At Level 18, the game introduces a paradigm shift, emphasizing not only immediate gains but also the importance of planning for the distant future. Starting a retirement account becomes a focal point, representing a forward-thinking approach to wealth accumulation. This quest is not merely about accumulating in-game currency; it's about securing a comfortable and prosperous endgame for your character.

The retirement account, akin to a sacred vault, serves as a repository for in-game wealth with a specific purpose—building a nest egg for the golden years. The choice between a traditional or Roth IRA mirrors the diverse playstyles available in the game, each with its unique advantages and considerations.

Opting for a traditional IRA allows your character to defer taxes on the contributed amount, presenting an immediate advantage. However, taxes will be levied upon withdrawal during the retirement phase.

On the other hand, a Roth IRA involves contributing after-tax income, offering the advantage of tax-free withdrawals in retirement—a strategic move that aligns with the game's principle of minimizing tax burdens.

The game underscores the importance of time as a valuable currency, especially when it comes to retirement savings. By initiating a retirement account at Level 18, your character capitalizes on the exponential growth potential facilitated by compound interest over an extended period. This strategic move leverages time as a powerful ally, showcasing the potential for substantial wealth accumulation by the time retirement beckons.

Choosing the right investment strategy within the retirement account adds another layer of complexity to this quest. The game offers diverse character playstyles, and your investment choices should align with your character's risk tolerance and long-term goals. Whether you opt for a growth-oriented strategy, delve into real estate investments, or adopt a defensive dividend approach, the retirement account becomes the canvas for crafting your character's financial masterpiece.

The strategic significance of starting a retirement account extends beyond the immediate benefits of wealth accumulation. It's a move that reflects a character's foresight, acknowledging the inevitability of the retirement phase and preparing accordingly. The retirement account serves as a testament to your character's commitment to financial well-being, transcending the whims of short-term gains for the enduring rewards of long-term wealth.

In conclusion, Level 18 heralds the quest of starting a retirement account, a strategic move that underscores the importance of foresight and planning in the wealth-building game. Whether choosing a traditional or Roth IRA, this quest sets in motion a trajectory toward long-term prosperity, leveraging the power of compound interest and prudent investment choices. By embarking on this quest, your character not only accumulates wealth but also fortifies its financial standing, ensuring a prosperous and secure endgame in the complex landscape of the wealth-building game.

The Stonk Strategy

As your character advances to Level 18 and beyond in the teen investment journey, the wealth-building game introduces an intricate quest known as "The Stonk Strategy." This quest revolves around understanding different investment approaches—an essential skill set that empowers your character to navigate the complex landscape of financial markets.

6.1 Understanding Different Investment Approaches

"The Stonk Strategy" emerges as a multifaceted quest that delves into the diverse playstyles available within the wealth-building game. Just as characters possess unique skills and abilities, investors have varied approaches to growing their in-game wealth. This quest acts as a guide, providing insights into the intricacies of different investment methodologies.

The first playstyle within "The Stonk Strategy" involves becoming a Growth Stock Wizard. This character archetype thrives on identifying companies with substantial growth potential. These are often young, dynamic firms poised for rapid expansion, mirroring the agility and ambition characteristic of a wizard on a quest. Investors adopting this approach focus on capitalizing on the upward trajectory of these stocks, aiming for significant returns over time.

In contrast, the Real Estate Investment Mage embodies a different aspect of "The Stonk Strategy." This playstyle revolves around leveraging the power of real estate—a tangible and often lucrative asset class within the game. Real Estate Investment Mages strategically acquire properties, aiming for rental income and potential appreciation. The quest involves mastering the nuances of property evaluation, market trends, and the art of generating passive income through real estate holdings.

The Defensive Dividend Investor, another character archetype within "The Stonk Strategy," adopts a more conservative playstyle. This investor seeks stable and established companies known for consistently paying dividends. The quest involves creating a diversified portfolio that provides a steady stream of income, mirroring the defensive stance of an investor safeguarding against market volatility.

"The Stonk Strategy" also acknowledges the significance of time-tested principles found in the teachings of legendary characters like Benjamin Graham. Investors looking to delve into advanced gameplay may embark on the quest of adopting value investing principles. The Intelligent Investor by Benjamin Graham serves as a valuable guide, imparting insights into selecting undervalued assets and building a robust, long-term investment strategy.

Understanding the dynamic character playstyles within "The Stonk Strategy" is essential for crafting a personalized approach to wealth-building. Each quest comes with its own risks, rewards, and intricacies, catering to diverse player preferences and risk appetites. The game encourages investors to explore these different approaches, gaining experience and expertise along the way.

In conclusion, "The Stonk Strategy" unfolds as a pivotal quest within the teen investment journey, providing a comprehensive guide to understanding different investment approaches. Whether aspiring to be a Growth Stock Wizard, a Real Estate Investment Mage, a Defensive Dividend Investor, or a follower of value investing principles, this quest empowers characters to align their investment strategies with their unique preferences and goals. As the wealth-building game evolves, mastering "The Stonk Strategy" becomes a key element in optimizing your character's financial journey.

As your character progresses through the levels of the teen investment journey, the quest for success takes a pivotal turn in "Selecting Stocks and Strategies." This quest within the wealth-building game becomes a crucial exploration into the art and science of choosing the right stocks and crafting strategies that align with your character's financial goals.

6.2 The Art of Stock Selection

The first segment of this quest revolves around mastering the art of stock selection—a skill set that separates successful players from the rest. In the intricate marketplace of the game, stocks represent the building blocks of wealth, and choosing them wisely is akin to selecting powerful tools for your character's arsenal.

Understanding the fundamentals of companies becomes paramount in this quest. Investors delve into financial statements, assessing metrics like revenue growth, profitability, and debt levels. This analytical approach empowers characters to identify stocks with strong foundations, aligning with the principle of making informed decisions in the game.

Another facet of the art of stock selection involves evaluating the competitive landscape. Successful players conduct thorough research on industries, identifying trends, and foreseeing potential disruptors. This strategic foresight mirrors a player's ability to anticipate and navigate challenges within the game, ensuring that the selected stocks align with the evolving dynamics of the in-game economy.

Crafting Strategies for Success

The second phase of the quest focuses on crafting strategies tailored to your character's unique playstyle and risk tolerance. This involves aligning your investment approach with overarching goals— whether they be short-term gains, long-term wealth accumulation, or a balanced combination of both.

For the Growth Stock Wizard, the strategy revolves around identifying companies with substantial growth potential. This quest involves staying attuned to market trends, technological advancements, and disruptive innovations. The goal is to capitalize on the upward trajectory of these dynamic stocks, mirroring the adventurous spirit of a wizard embarking on a quest for riches.

The Real Estate Investment Mage adopts a different strategy, emphasizing the acquisition and management of real estate assets. This quest involves meticulous property evaluation, understanding local market dynamics, and leveraging rental income as a consistent revenue stream. The strategy mirrors the mage's focus on tangible assets within the game.

Defensive Dividend Investors craft strategies centered around stable income from dividends. This involves building a diversified portfolio of companies with a history of consistent dividend payments. The quest aligns with the defensive stance of an investor seeking a reliable income stream, akin to fortifying a character against market volatility.

Understanding the nuances of these strategies enables players to navigate the diverse landscape of the wealth-building game effectively. It's not merely about selecting stocks randomly but about weaving them into a comprehensive strategy that aligns with your character's unique journey.

In conclusion, "Selecting Stocks and Strategies for Success" emerges as a pivotal quest within the teen investment journey, emphasizing the art of stock selection and the crafting of personalized strategies. Mastering this quest empowers players to make informed decisions, strategically aligning their portfolios with overarching financial goals. As the wealth-building game evolves, the ability to select stocks wisely and craft effective strategies becomes a defining element in ensuring your character's success in the dynamic landscape of financial markets.

Building Good Habits

As your character progresses through the levels of the teen investment journey, the quest for financial mastery takes a profound turn in the realm of building good habits. One of the fundamental habits that can shape your character's financial destiny is the art of tracking expenses—an essential skill set that cultivates financial awareness and lays the groundwork for prudent wealth management.

7.1 The Essence of Tracking Expenses

In the expansive world of the wealth-building game, every in-game currency earned and spent is a strategic move that shapes the character's financial trajectory. The quest for financial awareness begins with the meticulous tracking of expenses, transcending mere number-crunching to become a transformative habit that offers unparalleled insights into your character's financial landscape.

Tracking expenses serves as the cornerstone of financial awareness, akin to unveiling the fog-covered map of the game. Every expenditure, from in-game coffee purchases to strategic investments, is recorded and analyzed. This meticulous tracking empowers your character to gain a comprehensive understanding of where the in-game currency is flowing and the impact of each financial decision.

The Benefits of Financial Awareness

The habit of tracking expenses fosters a heightened sense of financial consciousness. Your character becomes attuned to spending patterns, identifying areas where resources are allocated wisely and recognizing potential leaks in the financial armor. This newfound awareness transforms the game from a mere financial journey into a strategic expedition where each expenditure is a calculated move toward wealth accumulation.

Moreover, financial awareness cultivates a proactive approach to wealth management. Characters equipped with this habit are better positioned to set and achieve financial goals. Whether it's accumulating in-game currency for a significant purchase, embarking on a quest to build an emergency fund, or strategically investing for long-term growth, the insights derived from tracking expenses become the compass guiding your character's financial endeavors.

The Practical Implementation

Implementing the habit of tracking expenses can take various forms, catering to different player preferences. Some characters prefer the hands-on approach of manual tracking, where each in-game currency transaction is meticulously recorded in a ledger or a designated journal. This method fosters a tactile connection to financial decisions, emphasizing the importance of each entry.

For characters who prefer a more streamlined approach, the game offers digital tools and apps that automate the tracking process. Apps like Mint or Personal Capital seamlessly integrate with the character's financial accounts, categorizing expenditures and providing real-time insights into spending patterns. This digital quest for financial awareness aligns with the modern, tech-savvy player's preferences, offering convenience and efficiency.

In conclusion, "Tracking Expenses for Financial Awareness" emerges as a transformative quest within the teen investment journey, underscoring the importance of building the foundational habit of financial tracking. This habit serves as a beacon of light in the intricate landscape of the wealth-building game, offering characters unparalleled insights, fostering financial awareness, and shaping the trajectory toward long-term wealth mastery. As the journey unfolds, characters armed with the habit of tracking expenses are better equipped to navigate the dynamic challenges and opportunities that define the ever-evolving game of wealth accumulation.

7.2 Prioritizing Health and Fitness

As your character advances through the levels of the teen investment journey, the quest for financial mastery expands to encompass a holistic approach—prioritizing health and fitness. In the intricate game of life, where every decision contributes to your character's overall well-being, this quest emerges as a transformative journey toward nurturing vitality and ensuring sustained success.

In the bustling world of the wealth-building game, the character's vitality is their most valuable asset. The quest for prioritizing health and fitness recognizes that optimal physical well-being is not just a side quest but an integral component of the main storyline. This quest transcends the narrow focus on accumulating in-game currency and unveils the interconnected nature of financial prosperity and personal vitality.

The essence lies in acknowledging that a healthy character is a formidable player in the game of life. Just as accumulating wealth requires strategic planning and execution, maintaining health and fitness demands intentional choices and consistent effort. The quest encourages characters to view their bodies as valuable resources, recognizing that a well-nurtured character can navigate the challenges of the game with resilience and vigor.

Benefits Beyond the Game

Prioritizing health and fitness extends its benefits far beyond the boundaries of the wealth-building game. The physical and mental well-being gained through this quest becomes the character's secret weapon, enhancing their overall quality of life. Characters who embark on this journey experience increased energy levels, improved focus, and heightened resilience to the inevitable twists and turns encountered in the game.

Moreover, the quest for health and fitness aligns with the principle of delayed gratification—an essential skill in the financial mastery playbook. Characters who invest time and effort in maintaining their health understand that the rewards, much like compound interest, accrue over time. This quest becomes a testament to the character's ability to balance immediate desires with long-term well-being, mirroring the strategic approach required for financial success.

Practical Implementation of the Quest

The quest for health and fitness takes on various forms, allowing characters to tailor their approach based on individual preferences and playstyles. Physical exercise becomes a cornerstone of this quest, offering characters the opportunity to enhance strength, endurance, and overall fitness. Whether it's engaging in cardiovascular activities, strength training, or immersive quests like yoga, the options are diverse, catering to different player preferences.

Nutritional choices form another vital aspect of this quest. Characters discover the power of nourishing their bodies with wholesome, nutrient-dense foods—a fuel that propels them through the challenges of the game. The quest emphasizes the importance of a balanced diet, aligning with the principle of diversification in both financial and health portfolios.

In conclusion, "Prioritizing Health and Fitness" emerges as a transformative quest within the teen investment journey, recognizing that true wealth encompasses not only financial prosperity but also the vitality of the character. This holistic approach integrates physical and mental well-being into the overarching narrative of success, positioning characters to thrive in both the wealth-building game and the larger adventure of life. As the journey unfolds, characters who prioritize health and fitness become resilient players, equipped to navigate the dynamic landscape of challenges and opportunities with a vitality that transcends the boundaries of the game.

7.3 Embracing Frugality and Delaying Gratification

As your character advances through the levels of the teen investment journey, a pivotal quest awaits— Embracing Frugality and Delaying Gratification. This quest, often considered the cornerstone of financial mastery, invites characters to master the art of resource allocation, challenging the conventional notions of immediate indulgence for the sake of long-term prosperity.

The Essence of Embracing Frugality

In the bustling world of the wealth-building game, where in-game currency flows and choices abound, the quest for frugality is not about deprivation but about strategic decision-making. Embracing frugality entails a deliberate and mindful approach to spending, recognizing that every coin expended today has a potential impact on the character's financial future.

The essence lies in fostering a mindset that values long-term goals over momentary pleasures. Characters undertaking this quest become adept at distinguishing between needs and wants, understanding that not every in-game desire warrants immediate fulfillment. This shift in perspective empowers characters to allocate resources judiciously, ensuring that every expenditure aligns with overarching financial objectives.

The Power of Delayed Gratification

At the heart of this quest lies the mastery of delayed gratification—a skill that sets characters on a trajectory toward sustained financial success. Delayed gratification involves forgoing immediate rewards for more significant, long-term gains. Characters who embrace this concept understand that the journey toward wealth is a marathon, not a sprint, and that strategic patience yields compounding benefits over time.

The quest emphasizes the importance of setting and prioritizing financial goals. Characters learn to differentiate between short-term pleasures and enduring achievements, aligning their choices with a vision of prosperity that extends far beyond the immediate horizon. This skill mirrors the strategic approach required for successful wealth accumulation, where each decision contributes to the character's financial narrative.

Practical Implementation of the Quest

Embracing frugality and delaying gratification involves practical, actionable steps that characters can integrate into their daily lives. Budgeting becomes a fundamental tool in this quest, enabling characters to allocate in-game currency intentionally. By creating a comprehensive budget, characters gain a clear understanding of their financial inflows and outflows, paving the way for informed spending decisions.

Characters undertaking this quest also explore alternative avenues for enjoyment that align with frugal principles. This could involve discovering low-cost or free activities, harnessing creativity to derive pleasure from simple experiences, and cultivating a mindset that finds fulfillment beyond material possessions. The quest encourages characters to savor the journey of wealth-building, finding joy in the strategic allocation of resources rather than succumbing to impulsive spending.

In conclusion, "Embracing Frugality and Delaying Gratification" emerges as a transformative quest within the teen investment journey, challenging characters to rethink their approach to spending and fostering a mindset that prioritizes strategic resource allocation. This quest goes beyond financial implications, shaping characters into prudent decision-makers who understand the power of delayed gratification in achieving enduring success. As the journey unfolds, characters who master this quest become architects of their financial destiny, strategically navigating the dynamic landscape of the wealth-building game with a vision that extends far into the future.

Bonus Cheat Codes

8.1 Utilizing Custodial Accounts

As characters progress through the intricate levels of the teen investment journey, seeking every possible advantage becomes paramount. Enter the Bonus Cheat Code—Utilizing Custodial Accounts. This strategic move allows characters to level up their financial game, leveraging the wisdom and experience of their in-game mentors, commonly known as parents.

The Significance of Custodial Accounts

In the expansive landscape of wealth-building strategies, custodial accounts emerge as a powerful tool for characters fortunate enough to have supportive in-game mentors, particularly parents. These accounts function as a bridge between generations, offering a unique opportunity for accelerated wealth growth by tapping into the experience and financial acumen of seasoned players.

The essence lies in the collaborative nature of custodial accounts. Younger characters can benefit from the established credit scores and financial stability of their in-game mentors, often resulting in favorable terms and opportunities. This strategic move reflects the principle of leveraging existing resources to enhance one's financial position—a concept integral to successful wealth accumulation.

Unlocking the Power of Custodial Accounts

The utilization of custodial accounts involves a collaborative effort between younger characters and their in-game mentors. The process typically begins with the younger character entrusting a portion of their hard-earned in-game currency to their mentor. In turn, the mentor invests these funds strategically, leveraging their experience to navigate the complexities of the in-game financial markets.

The collaboration extends to building and maintaining a robust credit history. By co-signing on the custodial account, the mentor imparts their positive credit history to the younger character, accelerating the establishment of a strong financial foundation. This bonus cheat code not only fast-tracks the accumulation of wealth but also instills valuable financial habits and discipline.

Practical Implementation of the Bonus Cheat Code

Young characters seeking to utilize custodial accounts can initiate discussions with their in-game mentors—usually parents—to explore this collaborative opportunity. Clear communication about financial goals, expectations, and the mechanics of the custodial account ensures a harmonious partnership. It's crucial to establish a level of trust and transparency to maximize the benefits of this bonus cheat code.

The mentor's role involves guiding investment decisions, sharing insights on financial strategies, and imparting valuable lessons learned through their own in-game experiences. This collaborative journey fosters a sense of shared responsibility and aligns the interests of both parties toward the common goal of accelerated wealth growth.

In conclusion, "Utilizing Custodial Accounts" stands as a bonus cheat code within the teen investment journey, presenting characters with a unique opportunity to leverage the experience and financial standing of their in-game mentors. This collaborative approach accelerates wealth growth, establishes a strong financial foundation, and imparts invaluable lessons for future financial endeavors. As characters strategically implement this bonus cheat code, they unlock a pathway to expedited success in the dynamic realm of the wealth-building game.

8.2 Joining a Community for Investment

As characters embark on the exhilarating quest of the teen investment journey, an often-overlooked bonus cheat code emerges—a dynamic force that transcends individual knowledge. Welcome to "Joining a Community for Investment Discussions," a strategic move that propels characters into a realm of collective wisdom, shared experiences, and unparalleled insights.

The Collective Intelligence Advantage

In the vast landscape of wealth-building, the power of collective intelligence becomes a formidable ally. Joining a community dedicated to investment discussions introduces characters to a diverse array of perspectives, strategies, and real-world anecdotes. This bonus cheat code transcends individual limitations, providing access to a wealth of knowledge derived from the collective experiences of a community of players.

The essence lies in the synergy of minds working towards a common goal. Investment communities serve as virtual arenas where characters can share successes, discuss challenges, and seek guidance from a pool of individuals with varying levels of expertise. This collaborative approach amplifies the learning curve, offering a 360-degree view of the dynamic financial landscape.

Navigating the Investment Landscape Together

The practical implementation of this bonus cheat code involves actively participating in investment communities tailored to the unique needs and interests of teen investors. Platforms such as Discord, Reddit, or specialized forums create spaces where characters can engage in meaningful discussions, ask questions, and learn from the triumphs and pitfalls of their peers.

Joining an investment community provides an avenue for characters to stay informed about market trends, discover new investment opportunities, and gain insights into effective wealth-building strategies. The diversity within these communities ensures exposure to a spectrum of investment styles, allowing characters to refine their own approaches based on collective wisdom.

Unlocking the Mentorship Dimension

Beyond the exchange of information, investment communities often foster mentorship dynamics. More experienced players willingly share their knowledge, offering guidance to those navigating the early stages of the wealth-building game. This mentorship dimension adds a valuable layer to the bonus cheat code, providing characters with personalized advice and insights tailored to their unique circumstances.

Community Accountability and Support

The bonus cheat code of joining an investment community extends beyond knowledge acquisition; it introduces an element of accountability and support. Engaging with a community encourages characters to set and track their financial goals, share progress, and seek advice during challenging moments. The collective support serves as a motivational force, reinforcing the commitment to the long-term objectives of wealth accumulation.

In conclusion, "Joining a Community for Investment Discussions" stands as a bonus cheat code that transcends the solitary nature of the teen investment journey. By actively participating in investment communities, characters unlock the power of collective intelligence, gain exposure to diverse perspectives, and navigate the complex wealth-building landscape with the support of a virtual mentorship network. This bonus cheat code transforms the journey from an individual quest into a collaborative adventure, enriching the overall experience and enhancing the probability of success in the dynamic realm of teen investments.

8.3 Claiming Free Stocks with WeBull and Robinhood

As characters traverse the intricate levels of the teen investment journey, discovering hidden bonus opportunities becomes a game-changing strategy. Among these elusive treasures are the enticing rewards offered by WeBull and Robinhood—two platforms that beckon with the promise of free stocks. Let's delve into the intricacies of "Claiming Free Stocks with WeBull and Robinhood," an alluring bonus cheat code that injects an extra boost into the wealth-building adventure.

The Temptation of Free Stocks

In the dynamic realm of wealth accumulation, the allure of free stocks adds a layer of excitement to the journey. WeBull and Robinhood, prominent players in the virtual marketplace, entice characters with the prospect of claiming stocks without the initial investment usually required in the stock market game. This bonus cheat code taps into the psychology of incentives, encouraging characters to explore these platforms and kickstart their investment ventures with a potential windfall.

Navigating WeBull's Bonus Landscape

WeBull, a leading brokerage platform, extends a generous offer to characters ready to embark on their investment odyssey. By leveraging this bonus cheat code, players can secure free stocks valued up to a substantial amount, depending on the prevailing promotional terms. The process involves signing up for a WeBull account, completing the necessary steps, and potentially receiving free stocks that can diversify and enhance one's investment portfolio.

Robinhood's Bounty of Free Stocks

Robinhood, another formidable player in the virtual investment arena, presents its own iteration of the bonus cheat code. New characters entering the game can claim free stocks upon signing up and fulfilling the platform's requirements. Robinhood's user-friendly interface and commission-free trading amplify the appeal of this bonus opportunity, providing an accessible entry point for those navigating the complexities of the stock market.

Practical Implementation for Aspiring Investors

The implementation of this bonus cheat code is straightforward yet impactful. Characters, whether seasoned or novice, can seize the opportunity by registering on both WeBull and Robinhood platforms. This strategic move not only diversifies the avenues for claiming free stocks but also aligns with the principle of maximizing available resources for accelerated wealth growth.

Strategic Considerations and Cautionary Insights

While claiming free stocks presents an enticing prospect, characters must approach this bonus cheat code with strategic considerations. Diversifying the investment landscape with free stocks introduces additional layers of risk and reward. It's crucial for players to conduct due diligence, research the offered stocks, and align their selections with their overall investment strategy.

Moreover, characters should exercise caution and refrain from succumbing to the allure of free stocks without a comprehensive understanding of the associated terms and conditions. Vigilance is the key to navigating this bonus cheat code successfully, ensuring that the claimed stocks contribute positively to the overall wealth-building objectives.

In conclusion, "Claiming Free Stocks with WeBull and Robinhood" emerges as a compelling bonus cheat code within the teen investment journey. By strategically leveraging the enticing offers from these platforms, characters inject additional momentum into their wealth-building quest. This bonus opportunity not only diversifies investment portfolios but also serves as a tangible reward for those navigating the complexities of the virtual stock market game. As characters claim their free stocks, they unlock new dimensions of the wealth-building adventure, propelling them closer to financial success in the dynamic realm of teen investments.

Conclusion

As our characters reach the conclusion of this comprehensive guide to teen investing, it's essential to reflect on the key strategies that pave the way for financial success.

The journey begins with the understanding that investing is a lifelong game, and starting early provides a significant advantage. From Level 13's emphasis on personal development to Level 18's essential items for success, each stage introduces crucial concepts. The importance of time, financial literacy through impactful books, and the initiation of financial accounts lay the groundwork. Practical aspects, such as obtaining a job, exploring passion through diverse activities, and discovering one's master skill, unfold as characters evolve through Levels 15 to 17.

The teen investment journey incorporates crucial financial tools like high-interest savings accounts, responsible credit card use, and the initiation of retirement accounts. The stonk strategy demystifies the complex world of stock market investments, guiding characters towards informed decisions. Building good habits, prioritizing health and fitness, and embracing frugality become character traits that lead to sustained financial well-being.

As characters absorb the wealth of information presented in this guide, the emphasis is not solely on accumulating riches but on enjoying the journey. Wealth-building is a dynamic adventure with its ups and downs, successes, and lessons. Moving forward, characters are encouraged to relish every level, embracing the experiences that shape them. It's a reminder that while financial success is a destination, the journey itself holds invaluable lessons and moments.

In conclusion, armed with a comprehensive understanding of financial strategies, our characters are well-equipped to navigate the teen investment landscape. The guide's parting wisdom is a call to not only build wealth but to savor the journey, fostering a balanced approach to life and finances.

May each character embark on their financial quest with confidence, resilience, and a sense of adventure. The teen investment journey is not just a game; it's an opportunity for growth, learning, and the creation of a prosperous future.

www.ingramcontent.com/pod-product-compliance
Lightning Source LLC
Chambersburg PA
CBHW071210290526
45796CB00008B/207